MW01177920

I care.
May this pure and simple message of hope lift you up today.

To: Bob and Glen

From: Danny & Edna

Date: April 14, 1996

PEACE *that defies* PAIN

MAX LUCADO

WORD PUBLISHING
Dallas · London · Vancouver · Melbourne

Peace That Defies Pain

Published by Word Publishing

ISBN 08499-5211-5

Printed in the United States of America

For information about "UpWords" radio ministry featuring Max Lucado, write:

P. O. Box 5860
San Antonio, TX 78201

Peace That Defies Pain

WE DON'T like to admit it, but pain is a fact of life. Sooner or later the "p" word comes into everyone's path. And when it does how do you deal with it?

Do you let pain conquer your spirit, or do you stare it down, armed with a "stubborn joy"?

Even in pain God is near. He wants you to grasp the peace that defies pain. He wants to be with you, facing pain with his holy joy.

Only he can show you the path to a defiant peace.

Chapter One

Sacred Delight

SHE HAS every reason to be bitter. Though talented, she went unrecognized for years. Prestigious opera circles closed their ranks when she tried to enter. American critics ignored her compelling voice. She was repeatedly rejected for parts for which she easily qualified. It was only after she went to Europe and won the hearts of tough-to-please European audiences that stateside opinion leaders acknowledged her talent.

Not only has her professional life been a battle, her personal life has been marked by challenge. She is the mother of two handicapped children, one of whom is severely retarded. Years ago, in order to escape the pace of New York City, she purchased a home on Martha's Vineyard. It burned to the ground two days before she was to move in.

Professional rejection. Personal setbacks. Perfect soil for the seeds of bitterness. A receptive field for the roots of resentment. But in this case, anger found no home.

Her friends don't call her bitter; they call her "Bubbles."

Beverly Sills. Internationally acclaimed opera singer. Retired director of the New York City Opera.

Her phrases are sugared with laughter. Her face is softened with serenity. Upon interviewing her, Mike Wallace stated that "she is one of the most impressive—if not *the* most impressive—ladies I've ever interviewed."

How can a person handle such professional rejection and personal trauma and still be known as Bubbles? "I choose to be cheerful," she says. "Years ago I knew I had little or no choice about success, circumstances or even happiness; but I knew I could choose to be cheerful."

"We have prayed for healing. God has not given it. But he has blessed us."

Glyn spoke slowly. Partly because of her conviction. Partly because of her disease. Her husband, Don, sat in the chair next to her. The three of us had come together to plan a funeral—hers. And now, with that task done, with the hymns selected and the directions given, Glyn spoke.

"He has given us strength we did notknow. He gave it when we needed it and not before." Her words were slurred, but clear. Her eyes were moist, but confident.

I wondered what it would be like to have my life taken from me at age forty-five. I wondered what it would be like to say good-bye to my children and spouse. I wondered what it would be like to be a witness to my own death.

"God has given us peace in our pain. He covers us all the time. Even when we are out of control, he is still there."

It had been a year since Glyn and Don had learned of Glyn's condition—amyotrophic lateral sclerosis (Lou Gehrig's disease). The cause and the cure remain a mystery. But the result doesn't. Muscle strength and mobility steadily deteriorate, leaving only the mind and the faith.

And it was the coming together of Glyn's mind and faith that caused me to realize I was doing more than planning a funeral. I was beholding holy jewels she had quarried out of the mine of despair.

"We can use any tragedy as a stumbling block or a stepping stone. . . .

"I hope this will not cause my family to be bitter. I hope I can be an example that God is wanting us to trust in the good times and the bad. For if we don't trust when times are tough, we don't trust at all."

Don held her hand. He wiped her tears. He wiped his own.

"Who are these two?" I asked myself as I watched him touch a tissue to her cheek. "Who are these, who, on the edge of life's river, can look across with such faith?"

The moment was solemn and sweet. I said little. One is not bold in the presence of the sacred.

❧

"I have everything I need for joy!" Robert Reed said. "Amazing!" I thought.

His hands are twisted and his feet are useless. He can't bathe himself. He can't feed himself. He can't brush his teeth, comb his hair, or put on his underwear. His shirts are held together by strips of Velcro®. His speech drags like a worn-out audio cassette.

Robert has cerebral palsy.

The disease keeps him from driving a car, riding a bike, and going for a walk. But it didn't keep him from graduating from high school or attending Abilene Christian University, from which he graduated with a degree in Latin. Having cerebral palsy didn't keep him from teaching at a St. Louis junior college or from venturing overseas on five mission trips.

And Robert's disease didn't prevent him from becoming a missionary in Portugal.

He moved to Lisbon, alone, in 1972. There he rented a hotel room and began studying Portuguese. He found a restaurant owner who would feed him after the rush hour and a tutor who would instruct him in the language.

Then he stationed himself daily in a park, where he distributed brochures about Christ. Within six years he led seventy people to the Lord, one of whom became his wife, Rosa.

I heard Robert speak recently. I watched other men carry him in his wheelchair onto the platform. I watched them lay a Bible in his lap. I watched his stiff fingers force open the pages. And I watched people in the audience wipe away tears of admiration from their faces. Robert could have asked for sympathy or pity, but he did just the opposite. He held his bent hand up in the air and boasted, "I have everything I need for joy."

His shirts are held together by Velcro®, but his life is held together by joy.

❧

No man had more reason to be miserable than this one—yet no man was more joyful.

His first home was a palace. Servants were at his fingertips. The snap of his fingers changed the course of history. His name was known and loved. He had everything—wealth, power, respect.

And then he had nothing.

Students of the event still ponder it. Historians stumble as they attempt to explain it. How could a king lose everything in one instant?

One moment he was royalty; the next he was in poverty.

His bed became, at best, a borrowed pallet—and usually the hard earth. He never owned even the most basic mode of transportation and was dependent upon handouts for his income. He was sometimes so hungry he would eat raw grain or pick fruit off a tree. He knew what it was like to be rained on, to be cold. He knew what it meant to have no home.

His palace grounds had been spotless; now he was exposed to filth. He had never known disease, but was now surrounded by illness.

In his kingdom he had been revered; now he was ridiculed. His neighbors tried to lynch him. Some called him a lunatic. His family tried to confine him to their house.

Those who didn't ridicule him tried to use him. They wanted favors. They wanted tricks. He was a novelty. They wanted to be seen with him—that is, until being with him was out of fashion. Then they wanted to kill him.

He was accused of a crime he never committed. Witnesses were hired to lie. The jury was rigged. No lawyer was assigned to his defense. A judge swayed by politics handed down the death penalty.

They killed him.

He left as he came—penniless. He was buried in a borrowed grave, his funeral financed by compassionate friends. Though he once had everything, he died with nothing.

He should have been miserable. He should have been bitter. He had every right to be a pot of boiling anger. But he wasn't.

He was joyful.

Sourpusses don't attract a following. People followed him wherever he went.

Children avoid soreheads. Children scampered after this man.

Crowds don't gather to listen to the woeful. Crowds clamored to hear him.

Why? He was joyful. He was joyful when he was poor. He was joyful when he was abandoned. He was joyful when he was betrayed. He was even joyful as he hung on a tool of torture, his hands pierced with six-inch Roman spikes.

Jesus embodied a stubborn joy. A joy that refused to bend in the wind of hard times. A joy that held its ground against pain. A joy whose roots extended deep into the bedrock of eternity.

Perhaps that's where Beverly Sills learned it. Without doubt, that is where Glyn Johnson and Robert Reed learned it. And that is where we can learn it.

What type of joy is this? What is this cheerfulness that dares to wink at adversity? What is this bird that sings while it is still dark? What is the source of this peace that defies pain?

I call it sacred delight.

It is sacred because it is not of the earth. What is sacred is God's. And this joy is God's.

It is delight because delight can both satisfy and surprise.

Delight is the Bethlehem shepherds dancing a jig outside a cave. Delight is Mary watching God sleep in a feed trough. Delight is white-haired Simeon praising God, who is about to be circumcised. Delight is Joseph teaching the Creator of the world how to hold a hammer.

Delight is the look on Andrew's face at the lunch pail that never came up empty. Delight is the dozing wedding guests who drank the wine that had been water. Delight is Jesus walking through waves as casually as you walk through curtains. Delight is a leper seeing a finger where there had been only a nub . . . a widow hosting a party with food made for a funeral . . . a paraplegic doing somersaults. Delight is Jesus doing impossible things in crazy ways: healing the blind with spit, paying taxes with a coin found in a fish's mouth, and coming back from the dead disguised as a gardener.

What is sacred delight? It is God doing what gods would be doing only in your wildest dreams—wearing diapers, riding donkeys, washing feet, dozing in storms. Delight is the day they accused God of having too much fun, attending too many parties, and spending too much time with the Happy Hour crowd.

Delight is the day's wage paid to workers who had worked only one hour . . . the father scrubbing the pig smell off his son's back . . . the shepherd throwing a party because the sheep was found. Delight is a discovered pearl, a multiplied talent, a heaven-bound beggar, a criminal in the kingdom. Delight is the surprise on the faces of street folks who have been invited to a king's banquet.

Delight is the Samaritan woman big-eyed and speechless, the adulteress walking out of the stone-cluttered courtyard, and a skivvy-clad Peter plunging into cold waters to get close to the one he'd cursed.

Sacred delight is good news coming through the back door of your heart. It's what you'd always dreamed but never expected. It's the too-good-to-be-true coming true. It's having God as your pinch-hitter, your lawyer, your dad, your biggest fan, and your best friend. God on your side, in your heart, out in front, and protecting your back. It's hope where you least expected it: a flower in life's sidewalk.

It is *sacred* because only God can grant it. It is a *delight* because it thrills. Since it is sacred, it can't be stolen. And since it is delightful, it can't be predicted.

It was this gladness that danced through the Red Sea. It was this joy that blew the trumpet at Jericho. It was this secret that made Mary sing. It was this surprise that put the springtime into Easter morning.

It is God's gladness. It's sacred delight.

And it is this sacred delight that Jesus promises in the Sermon on the Mount.

Nine times he promises it. And he promises it to an unlikely crowd:

- *"The poor in spirit."* Beggars in God's soup kitchen.
- *"Those who mourn."* Sinners Anonymous bound together by the truth of their introduction: "Hi, I am me. I'm a sinner."

- *"The meek."* Pawnshop pianos played by Van Cliburn. (He's so good no one notices the missing keys.)
- *"Those who hunger and thirst."* Famished orphans who know the difference between a TV dinner and a Thanksgiving feast.
- *"The merciful."* Winners of the million-dollar lottery who share the prize with their enemies.
- *"The pure in heart."* Physicians who love lepers and escape infection.
- *"The peacemakers."* Architects who build bridges with wood from a Roman cross.
- *"The persecuted."* Those who manage to keep an eye on heaven while walking through hell on earth.

It is to this band of pilgrims that God promises a special blessing. A heavenly joy. A sacred delight.

But this joy is not cheap. What Jesus promises is not a gimmick to give you goose bumps nor a mental attitude that has to be pumped up at pep rallies. No, Matthew 5 describes God's radical reconstruction of the heart.

Observe the sequence. First, we recognize we are in need (we're poor in spirit). Next, we repent of our self-sufficiency (we mourn). We quit calling the shots and surrender control to God (we're meek). So grateful are we for his presence that we yearn for more of him (we hunger and thirst). As we grow closer to him, we become more like him. We forgive others (we're merciful). We change our outlook (we're pure in heart). We love others (we're peacemakers). We endure injustice (we're persecuted).

It's no casual shift of attitude. It is a demolition of the old structure and a creation of the new. The more radical the change, the greater the joy. And it's worth every effort, for this is the joy of God.

It's no accident that the same word used by Jesus to promise sacred delight is the word used by Paul to describe God:

"The blessed God . . ."[1]

"God, the blessed and only Ruler . . ."[2]

Think about God's joy. What can cloud it? What can quench it? What can kill it? Is God ever in a bad mood because of bad weather? Does God get ruffled over long lines or traffic jams? Does God ever refuse to rotate the earth because his feelings are hurt?

No. His is a joy which consequences cannot quench. His is a peace which circumstances cannot steal.

There is a delicious gladness that comes from God. A holy joy. A sacred delight.

And it is within your reach. You are one decision away from joy.

Chapter Two

Seeing God Through Shattered Glass

THERE IS a window in your heart through which you can see God. Once upon a time the window was clear. Your view of God was crisp. You could see God as vividly as you could see a gentle valley or hillside. The glass was clean, the pane unbroken.

You knew God. You knew how he worked. You knew what he wanted you to do. No surprises. Nothing unexpected. You knew that God had a will, and you continually discovered what it was.

Then, suddenly, the window cracked. A pebble broke the window. A pebble of pain.

Perhaps the stone struck when you were a child and a parent left home—forever. Maybe the rock hit in adolescence when your heart was broken. Maybe you made it into adulthood before the window was cracked. But then the pebble came.

Was it a phone call? "We have your daughter at the station. You'd better come down."

Was it a letter on the kitchen table? "I've left. Don't try to reach me. Don't try to call me. It's over. I just don't love you anymore."

Was it a diagnosis from the doctor? "I'm afraid our news is not very good."

Was it a telegram? "We regret to inform you that your son is missing in action."

Whatever the pebble's form, the result was the same—a shattered window. The pebble missiled into the pane and shattered it. The crash echoed down the halls of your heart. Cracks shot out from the point of impact, creating a spider web of fragmented pieces.

And suddenly God was not so easy to see. The view that had been so crisp had changed. You turned to see God, and his figure was distorted. It was hard to see him through the pain. It was hard to see him through the fragments of hurt.

You were puzzled. God wouldn't allow something like this to happen, would he? Tragedy and travesty weren't on the agenda of the One you had seen, were they? Had you been fooled? Had you been blind?

The moment the pebble struck, the glass became a reference point for you. From then on, there was life before the pain and life after the pain. Before your pain, the view was clear; God seemed so near. After your pain, well, he was harder to see. He seemed a bit distant . . . harder to perceive. Your pain distorted the view—not eclipsed it, but distorted it.

Maybe these words don't describe your situation. There are some people who never have to redefine or refocus their view of God. Most of us do.

Most of us know what it means to feel disappointed by God.

Most of us have a way of completing this sentence: "If God is God, then . . ." Call it an agenda, a divine job description. Each of us has an unspoken, yet definitive, expectation of what God should do. "If God is God, then . . ."

- There will be no financial collapse in my family.
- My children will never be buried before me.
- People will treat me fairly.
- This church will never divide.
- My prayer will be answered.

These are not articulated criteria. They are not written down or notarized. But they are real. They define the expectations we have of God. And when pain comes into our world—when the careening pebble splinters the window of our hearts—these expectations go unmet and doubts may begin to surface.

We look for God, but can't find him. Fragmented glass hinders our vision. He is enlarged through this piece and reduced through that one. Lines jigsaw their way across his face. Large sections of shattered glass opaque the view.

And now you aren't quite sure what you see.

❧

The disciples weren't sure what they saw, either.

Jesus failed to meet their expectations. The day Jesus fed the five thousand men he didn't do what they wanted him to do.

The Twelve returned from their mission followed by an army. They finished their training. They recruited the soldiers. They were ready for battle. They expected Jesus to let the crowds crown him as king and attack the city of Herod. They expected battle plans . . . strategies . . . a new era for Israel.

What did they get?

Just the opposite.

Instead of weapons, they got oars. Rather than being sent to fight, they were sent to float. The crowds were sent away. Jesus walked away. And they were left on the water with a storm brewing in the sky.

What kind of Messiah would do this?

Note carefully the sequence of the stormy evening as Matthew records it:

> Immediately Jesus made the disciples get into the boat and go on ahead of him to the other side, while he dismissed the crowd. After he had dismissed them, he went up on a mountainside by himself to pray. *When evening came* [emphasis mine], he was there alone, but the boat was already a considerable distance from land, buffeted by the waves because the wind was against it.[1]

Matthew is specific about the order of events. Jesus sent the disciples to the boat. Then he dismissed the crowd and ascended a mountainside. It was evening, probably around 6:00 P.M. The storm struck immediately. The sun had scarcely set before typhoon-like winds began to roar.

Note that Jesus sent the disciples out into the storm *alone.* Even as he was ascending the mountainside, he could feel and hear the gale's force. Jesus was not ignorant of the storm. He was aware that a torrent was coming that would carpet-bomb the sea's surface. But he didn't turn around. The disciples were left to face the storm . . . alone.

The greatest storm that night was not in the sky; it was in the disciples' hearts. The greatest fear was not from seeing the storm-driven waves; it came from seeing the back of their leader as he left them to face the night with only questions as companions.

It was this fury that the disciples were facing that night. Imagine the incredible strain of bouncing from wave to wave in a tiny fishing vessel. One hour would weary you. Two hours would exhaust you.

Surely Jesus will help us, they thought. They'd seen him still storms like this before. On this same sea, they had awakened him during a storm, and he had commanded the skies to be silent. They'd seen him quiet the wind and soothe the waves. *Surely he will come off the mountain.*

But he doesn't. Their arms begin to ache from rowing. Still no sign of Jesus. Three hours. Four hours. The winds rage. The boat bounces. Still no Jesus. Midnight comes. Their eyes search for God—in vain.

By now the disciples have been on the sea for as long as six hours.

All this time they have fought the storm and sought the Master. And, so far, the storm is winning. And the Master is nowhere to be found.

"Where is he?" cried one.

"Has he forgotten us?" yelled another.

"He feeds thousands of strangers and yet leaves us to die?" muttered a third.

The Gospel of Mark adds compelling insight into the disciples' attitude. "They had not understood about the loaves; their hearts were hardened."[2]

What does Mark mean? Simply this. The disciples were mad. They began the evening in a huff. Their hearts were hardened toward Jesus because he fed the multitude. Their preference, remember, had been to "send the crowds away."[3] And Jesus had told them to feed the people. But they wouldn't try. They said it couldn't be done. They told Jesus to let the people take care of themselves.

Also keep in mind that the disciples had just spent some time on center stage. They'd tasted stardom. They were celebrities. They had rallied crowds. They had recruited an army. They were, no doubt, pretty proud of themselves. With chests a bit puffy and heads a bit swollen, they'd told Jesus, "Just send them away."

Jesus didn't. Instead, he chose to bypass the reluctant disciples and use the faith of an anonymous boy. What the disciples said couldn't be done was done—in spite of them, not through them.

They pouted. They sulked. Rather than being amazed at the miracle, they became mad at the Master. After all, they had felt foolish passing out the very bread they said could not be made. Add to that Jesus' command to go to the boat when they wanted to go to battle, and it's easier to understand why these guys are burning!

"Now what is Jesus up to, leaving us out on the sea on a night like this?"

It's 1:00 A.M., no Jesus.

It's 2:00 A.M., no Jesus.

Peter, Andrew, James, and John have seen storms like this. They are fishermen; the sea is their life. They know the havoc the gale-force winds can wreak. They've seen the splintered hulls float to shore. They've attended the funerals. They know, better than anyone, that this night could be their last. "Why doesn't he come?" they sputter.

Finally, he does. "During the fourth watch of the night [3:00 to 6:00 A.M.] Jesus went out to them, walking on the lake."[4]

Jesus came. He finally came. But between verse 24—being buffeted by waves—and verse 25—when Jesus appeared—a thousand questions are asked.

Questions you have probably asked, too. Perhaps you know the angst of being suspended between verses 24 and 25. Maybe you're riding a storm, searching the coastline for a light, a glimmer of hope. You know that Jesus knows what you are going through. You know that he's aware of your storm. But as hard as you look to find him, you can't see him. Maybe your heart, like the disciples' hearts, has been hardened by unmet expectations. Your pleadings for help are salted with angry questions.

This booklet is for you if the pebble of pain has struck the window of your heart, if you've known the horror of looking for God's face and seen only his back as he ascends a mountainside.

When you can't see him, trust him. The figure you see is not a ghost. The voice you hear is not the wind.

Jesus is closer than you've ever dreamed.

Chapter Three

He Speaks Through the Storm

IT ALL HAPPENED in one day. One day he could choose his tee time at the nicest golf course in the country; the next he couldn't even be the caddie. One day he could Lear jet across the country to see the heavyweight bout at the Las Vegas Mirage. The next he couldn't afford a city bus across town.

Talk about calm becoming chaos . . .

The first thing to go is his empire. The market crashes; his assets tumble. What is liquid goes dry. What has been up goes down. Stocks go flat, and Job goes broke. There he sits in his leather chair and soon-to-be-auctioned-off mahogany desk when the phone rings with news of calamity number two:

The kids were at a resort for the holidays when a storm blew in and took them with it.

Shell-shocked and dumbfounded, Job looks out the window into the sky that seems to be getting darker by the minute. He starts praying, telling God that things can't get any worse . . . and that's exactly what happens. He feels a pain in his chest that is more than last night's ravioli. The next thing he knows, he is bouncing in an ambulance with wires stuck to his chest and needles stuck in his arm.

He ends up tethered to a heart monitor in a community hospital room. Next to him lies an illegal immigrant who can't speak English.

Not, however, that Job lacks for conversation.

First there is his wife. Who could blame her for being upset at the week's calamities? Who could blame her for telling Job to curse God? But to curse God *and die?* If Job doesn't already feel abandoned, you know he does the minute his wife tells him to pull the plug and be done with it.

Then there are his friends. They have the bedside manner of a drill sergeant and the compassion of a chain-saw killer. A revised version of their theology might read like this: "Boy, you must have done something really bad! We know that God is good, so if bad things are happening to you, then you have been bad. Period."

Does Job take that lying down? Not hardly.

"You are doctors who don't know what they are doing," he says. "Oh, please be quiet! That would be your highest wisdom."[2]

Translation? "Why don't you take your philosophy back to the pigpen where you learned it."

"I'm not a bad man," Job argues. "I paid my taxes. I'm active in civic duties. I'm a major contributor to United Way and a volunteer at the hospital bazaar."

Job is, in his eyes, a good man. And a good man, he reasons, deserves a good answer.

"Your suffering is for your own good," states Elihu, a young minister fresh out of seminary who hasn't lived long enough to be cynical and hasn't hurt enough to be quiet. He paces back and forth in the hospital room, with his Bible under his arm and his finger punching the air.

"God does all these things to a man—twice, even three times—to turn back his soul from the pit, that the light of life may shine on him."[3]

Job follows his pacing like you'd follow a tennis player, head turning from side to side. What the young man says isn't bad theology, but it isn't much comfort, either. Job steadily tunes him out and slides lower and lower under the covers. His head hurts. His eyes burn. His legs ache. And he can't stomach any more hollow homilies.

Yet his question still hasn't been answered: "God, why is this happening to me?"

So God speaks.

Out of the thunder, he speaks. Out of the sky, he speaks. For all of us who would put ditto marks under Job's question and sign our names to it, he speaks.

- For the father who holds a rose taken off his son's coffin, he speaks.
- For the wife who holds the flag taken off her husband's casket, he speaks.
- For the couple with the barren womb and the fervent prayers, he speaks.
- For any person who has tried to see God through shattered glass, he speaks.

- For those of us who have dared to say, "If God is God, then . . .," God speaks.

He speaks out of the storm and into the storm, for that is where Job is. That is where God is best heard.

God's voice thunders in the room. Elihu sits down. Job sits up. And the two will never be the same again.

"Who is this that darkens my counsel with words without knowledge?"[4]

Job doesn't respond.

"Brace yourself like a man; I will question you, and you shall answer me."[5]

"Where were you when I laid the foundations of the earth? Tell me, if you know so much."[6]

One question would have been enough for Job, but it isn't enough for God.

"Do you know how its dimensions were determined and who did the surveying?" God asks. "What supports its foundations, and who laid its cornerstone, as the morning stars sang together and all the angels shouted for joy?"[7]

Questions rush forth. They pour like sheets of rain out of the clouds. They splatter in the chambers of Job's heart with a wildness and a beauty and a terror that leave every Job who has ever lived drenched and speechless, watching the Master redefine who is who in the universe.

> Have you ever once commanded the morning to appear, and caused the dawn to rise in the east? Have you ever told the daylight to spread to the ends of the earth, to end the night's wickedness?[8]

God's questions aren't intended to teach; they are intended to stun. They aren't intended to enlighten; they are intended to awaken. They aren't intended to stir the mind; they are intended to bend the knees.

> Has the location of the gates of Death been revealed to you? Do you realize the extent of the earth? Tell me about it if you know! Where does the light come from, and how do you get there? Or tell me about the darkness. Where does it come from? Can you find its boundaries, or go to its source? But of course you know all this! For you were born before it was all created, and you are so very experienced![9]

Finally Job's feeble hand lifts, and God stops long enough for him to respond. "I am nothing—how could I ever find the answers? I lay my hand upon my mouth in silence. I have said too much already."[10]

God's message has connected:

- Job is a peasant, telling the King how to run the kingdom.
- Job is an illiterate, telling e. e. cummings to capitalize his personal pronouns.
- Job is the bat boy, telling Babe Ruth to change his batting stance.
- Job is the clay, telling the potter not to press so hard.

"I owe no one anything," God declares in the crescendo of the wind. "Everything under the heaven is mine."[11]

Job couldn't argue. God owes no one anything. No explanations. No excuses. No help.

God has no debt, no out-standing balance, no favors to return. God owes no man anything.

Which makes the fact that he gave us everything even more astounding.

❧

How you interpret this holy presentation is key. You can interpret God's hammering speech as a divine "in-your-face" tirade if you want. You can use the list of unanswerable questions to prove that God is harsh, cruel, and distant. You can use the Book of Job as evidence that God gives us questions and no answers. But to do so, you need some scissors. To do so, you need to cut out the rest of the Book of Job.

For that is not how Job heard it. All his life, Job had been a good man. All his life, he had believed in God. All his life, he had discussed God, had notions about him, and had prayed to him.

But in the storm Job sees him!

He sees Hope. Lover. Destroyer. Giver. Taker. Dreamer. Deliverer.

Job sees the tender anger of a God whose unending love is often received with peculiar mistrust. Job stands as a blade of grass against the consuming fire of God's splendor. Job's demands melt like wax as God pulls back the curtain and heaven's light falls uneclipsed across the earth.

Job sees God.

God could turn away at this point. The gavel has been slammed, the verdict has been rendered. The Eternal Judge has spoken.

Ah, but God is not angry with Job. Firm? Yes. Direct? No doubt. Clear and convincing? Absolutely. But angry? No.

God is never irritated by the candle of an honest seeker.

If you underline any passage in the Book of Job, underline this one: "I had heard about you before, but now I have seen you."[12]

Job sees God—and that is enough.

But it isn't enough for God.

The years to come find Job once again sitting behind his mahogany desk with health restored and profits up. His lap is once again full of children and grandchildren and great-grandchildren—for four generations!

If Job ever wonders why God doesn't bring back the children he had taken away, he doesn't ask. Maybe he doesn't ask because he knows that his children could never be happier than they are in the presence of this One he has seen so briefly.

Something tells me that Job would do it all again, if that's what it took to hear God's voice and stand in the Presence. Even if God left him with his bedsores and bills, Job would do it again.

For God gave Job more than Job ever dreamed. God gave Job Himself.

CHAPTER ONE
SACRED DELIGHT

Now when he saw the crowds, he went up on a mountainside and sat down. . . . and he began to teach them, saying: "Blessed . . ."

1. Describe the happiest moment you can remember. Jot down some of the circumstances surrounding it—who was involved, when it happened, how long your happiness lasted. Now, recall the time in your life that you were most miserable. What was happening then? How have the circumstances of your life contributed to your happiness or unhappiness?

2. What is the difference between "choosing to be cheerful," as Beverly Sills describes it, and putting on a cheerful facade to cover up or deny misery? Under what circumstances, if any, could "choosing to be cheerful" be a negative choice?

3. The following Old Testament passages reveal some of the ideas about happiness Jesus' listeners had grown up on. How does each passage describe a happy (blessed) person?

- Psalm 1:1–6
- Psalm 2:10–12
- Psalm 32:1–2, 5–7, 10–11

- Psalm 41:1–3
- Psalm 84:4–5, 11–12
- Psalm 94:12–13
- Psalm 112:1–9
- Proverbs 8:1–2, 32–36 (note who is "speaking")

4. Chapter 1 states that the Greek word Jesus used for "blessed' in the Beatitudes (*makarios*) is the same one used by Paul to describe God. It was used in other ancient literature to describe the "happy state of the gods above earthly sufferings" and to denote "a transcendent happiness of a life beyond care, labor and death" (*Theological Dictionary of the New Testament*, 4:362). What does Jesus' use of this powerful word say about the kind of happiness he is promising?

CHAPTER TWO
SEEING GOD THROUGH SHATTERED GLASS

1. Can you remember a time when pain shattered your expectations of God, when he did something that didn't seem right to you or gave you the opposite of what you thought you should receive? If so, how did that experience affect your view of God?

2. Do you have a phrase (or even several) that is always ready to complete this sentence: "If God is God, then . . ."? What is it? How did that phrase develop in your thinking?

3. Read Matthew 14:22–24. Describe a time when you felt alone in the storm—abandoned by God's protection and care. Did you become weary, even exhausted?

   How did you feel about God during that time? In what ways was your heart, like the hearts of the disciples, hardened against him? (See Mark 6:52.)

4. Has God ever used an exhausting, painful, or seemingly impossible circumstance to teach you something about himself or your relationship with him? If so, describe the circumstance and the lesson.

5. In what areas of your life could you trust God more, rather than questioning how he seems to be working?

   When the next storm in your life appears, how can you be better prepared to see Jesus at work in the midst of the storm?

CHAPTER THREE
HE SPEAKS THROUGH THE STORM

1. Describe the most difficult circumstance you've ever faced. Who was involved? What happened? How long did it last?

   Did you question or lash out at God during that time? What was the result?

   What did you learn through that experience? How did it affect your view of yourself? Of God? Of others?

2. Think about friends who "advised" you during a difficult time. What type of wisdom did they give you? What kind of

advice have you given to others who have faced difficult times?

3. Do you sometimes receive God's unending love with mistrust? Name a situation in which you believed that God's love wasn't in your best interest. What was the outcome?

4. Read Job 1:8–12; 2:3–7. Why did God allow Job's difficult circumstances to occur? How does that knowledge add perspective to what happened to Job? Does that knowledge shed any light on the suffering in your life or in the life of someone you know? If so, explain.

5. The author writes that God is "best heard in the storm." Do you agree? Why or why not?

6. Read Job 38–41. What is God's message to you in his answer to Job's questions?

7. When God finished speaking, Job said, "I had heard about you before, but now I have seen you" (Job 42:5, TLB). What did Job gain as a result of seeing God?

Notes

Chapter 1—Sacred Delight

1. Timothy 1:11.
2. 1 Timothy 6:15.

Chapter 2—Seeing God Through Shattered Glass

1. Matthew 14:22–24.
2. Mark 6:52.
3. Matthew 14:15
4. Ibid.

Chapter 3—He Speaks Through the Storm

1. Job 42:5, TLB
2. Job 13:4, 5, TLB
3. Job 33:29.
4. Job 38:2.
5. Job 38:3.
6. Job 38:4, TLB
7. Job 38:5-7, TLB
8. Job 38:12, 13, TLB
9. Job 38:17-21, TLB

10. Job 40:4, 5, TLB
11. Job 41:11, TLB
12. Job 42:5, TLB